Everything You Need to Know About Birth Order

The order in which we were born affects us during childhood, in our teen years, and as adults.

Everything You Need to Know About Birth Order

Katherine Krohn

The Rosen Publishing Group, Inc.
New York

This book is dedicated to Vicki.
"She rides in the front seat, she's my older sister . . ."
—Carly Simon

Published in 2000 by The Rosen Publishing Group, Inc.
29 East 21st Street, New York, NY 10010

First Edition

Library of Congress Cataloging-in-Publication Data

Krohn, Katherine.
  Everything you need to know about birth order / Katherine Krohn.
    p. cm.—(The need to know library)
  ISBN 0-8239-3228-1
  1. Birth order—Juvenile literature. [1. Birth order. 2. Brothers and sisters. 3. Parent and child.] I. Title. II. Series.
  BF723.B5 K76 2000
  155.9'24—dc21

                                                                00-008569

Manufactured in the United States of America

Contents

Introduction

Do you come from a large family with lots of brothers and sisters, or are you an only child? Are you the firstborn, the last born, or a middle child in your family? If you have brothers and sisters, how would your life be different if you were an only child? If you are an only child, what do you think it would be like to have siblings? Would you feel differently about yourself? How does our birth position—the order in which we were born—affect us during childhood, in the teen years, and when we are adults? This fascinating question, which is becoming more and more important to behavior researchers, is the subject of this book.

It has been known for a long time that factors such as genetics, parenting, and the home environment help shape a child's personality and behavior. But many psychologists now believe that another factor—birth order (your birth position in your family)—greatly affects who you are and how you approach the world.

Alfred Adler, a student of Sigmund Freud, first introduced the importance of birth order in 1908. Adler theorized that birth order plays a central role in shaping a child's emotional development and self-esteem. Psychologists who follow Adler's theory believe that birth order can influence your self-esteem, the roles you take in life, how happy or successful you are—and even who you will choose to date and marry!

"A person's family exerts more influence on him or her than any other organization, institution, or experience," says Dr. Kevin Leman, author of *The Birth Order Book*. Leman adds: "In any family, a person's order of birth has a lifelong effect on who and what that person turns out to be."

Each time a child is born, his or her parents are at a new level of experience and a new stage of life. Sometimes their economic situation or energy level varies dramatically. And it's not just the parents who are changing: Every time a new child is born, every member of the family changes. Essentially, the family reshapes itself.

The effects of birth order can be lasting. People can carry emotional wounds related to the birth order position into their adult relationships. For this reason, it's important while you are still young to understand the effects of your birth position. Gaining perspective on your place in your family and the difference it has made—and will make—in your life will be extremely helpful to you as you get older, meet new people, and begin a life independent of your parents. Read on to find out more about the fascinating study of birth order, what birth order means for others, and, most important, what it means for you.

Chapter One | Understanding the Effects of Birth Order

As you learned in the introduction, birth order can have a tremendous effect on how you relate to other people, how you choose your friends, and who you choose as a spouse. "I was the last child of six," recalls Julie. "I don't remember getting much affection as a child. My parents just weren't 'touchy-feely' people. Not surprisingly, I chose a husband who has a problem being affectionate."

In contrast, Gretchen was an only child. When she was born, her parents were financially well-to-do, in step with the latest child-raising techniques, and extremely affectionate with Gretchen. They gave her all the material things she wanted—within reason, of course. Gretchen could throw frequent parties and had many friends.

"I grew up feeling that the world was a bountiful, friendly place," says Gretchen. "I am so grateful that I

Only children, who receive all of their parents' attention, are often very secure and confident individuals.

was born to parents who really, really wanted a child. I felt very secure as a child as a result. And today—unless I'm having a very 'off' day—I am a very self-confident adult."

An Adlerian therapist would probably say that because Gretchen didn't have siblings, she didn't have to compete for parental attention. As a result, Gretchen grew up to have high self-esteem and a positive attitude.

What Is the "Best" Birth Order Position?

Gretchen is basically a happy, well-adjusted person, but did she have a "perfect" birth order situation? Of course not! There is no best birth order position. Although Gretchen's situation was ideal in some ways, it wasn't in others.

"Sometimes I feel lonely as an adult," says Gretchen. "We have very small family gatherings, and sometimes I wonder if I missed out on something. I'm a little sad that I won't have the experience of having siblings, and I won't have nieces or nephews."

Every birth order position has its advantages and disadvantages. Mark, sixteen, is a sophomore in high school. He is the oldest of three children. He has two younger sisters, ages thirteen and ten. Like many firstborns, Mark complains that his parents expect too much from him.

"My parents tell me I have to set a good example for my sisters. They expect me to get all A's in school. I feel like I have to be perfect. Sometimes it feels like a lot of pressure, but I don't want to let my parents down."

Although Mark feels pressure from his parents to set a good example for his siblings, there are positive things about his birth position. For instance, for the first three years of his life, before his sister Amy was born, Mark was an only child. He had his parents' and grandparents' undivided attention during those important early years. Also, Mark has the advantage of always being the first sibling to try new things.

Mark's sister Amy is a second-born. For three years she was the youngest in the family, enjoying the benefits of that birth position. Much to Mark's dismay, their parents showered her with attention. When their sister Wendy was born, Amy was dethroned as the baby of the family. Wendy was now the baby, and Amy was the middle child.

"I know I was very young when Wendy was born, but I can still remember feeling jealous that she got my clothes when I outgrew them," Amy says. "Which is kind of crazy of me because she says that she hated getting my hand-me-downs!"

Wendy, the youngest child in the family, has the birth order position of youngest child. Luckily for her, her parents have relaxed a bit in their parenting and they don't set as many rules for their youngest child. In

It can seem unfair when you are treated differently than your siblings.

fact, Wendy's older siblings claim that Wendy "gets away with murder." But Wendy tells a different story.

"I am ten years old, and my parents still call me 'the baby in the family'—I hate it! I never get to do anything that my older brother and sister get to do. And I have to go to bed an hour earlier than my sister and we share the same room! It's not fair!"

Twins and Birth Order Theory

What do Elvis Presley, artist Diego Rivera, and writer Thornton Wilder have in common? All had twin brothers who died at birth. "Losing a twin is losing a very special person, a very significant bond," says Chicago therapist Joseph Andres. "If a person knows that he or she had a twin—and lost that twin—it can give the person a sense of loss and even grief. The feelings can be lasting—sometimes lifelong."

Elvis's identical twin brother, Jesse Garon Presley, died at birth. Elvis's friends (as well as Elvis himself) have said that the singer was a lonely man. Did his lost twin create yearning and loneliness in Elvis's heart?

Twins have a unique birth order position, as twins can be both extremely competitive with one another and very close companions. In every pair of twins, one is born first, if only by a few minutes or seconds. The older twin is often the dominant twin or leader.

Regardless of the effects of birth order, most twins agree that their life is enriched by having a twin sibling. Famous twins include composer Johann Christian Bach, who had a twin brother named Johann Ambrosius. Twin sisters Abigail van Buren (of "Dear Abby" fame) and Ann Landers have both enjoyed successful careers as advice columnists.

What About Adopted Children and Stepchildren?

Did you know that writers Edward Albee and Jack London were both adopted? So were talk-show host Art Linkletter and former president Gerald Ford. How can being adopted influence the birth order experience?

Greg, now twenty-two, was adopted by a single mother when he was an infant. He didn't have any siblings with whom to share parental love and attention. He also didn't have a father. His mother could devote all of her time and energy to her adopted child.

"I know my mother really, really loved me and wanted me. I was the center of her universe. I can see now that I had a total lack of competition from brothers or sisters for any parental affection. Today I am a very well-adjusted person. Well, maybe too well adjusted! I have a big ego, I admit."

Stepchildren—children of divorced parents who remarry—are faced with a special challenge. They must adapt to a new family with its own unique circumstances. Mack was three and Karrie was six when their parents divorced. Within a year, their mother remarried and the children moved into their stepfather's home. "My stepfather had two little girls, ages four and five," says Mack. "Oddly enough, I don't remember there being a lot of jealousy or hard feelings. We were all pals, and we are still close today."

"A key factor in how successfully a stepfamily can build loving relationships is the age of the children at the time of the new marriage," says Dr. Kevin Leman. "If the children are young, the odds are much better. Their personalities are still being formed and time is on the parents' side. But suppose the children are older— for example, a ten-year-old girl is joined to a stepsister, thirteen, and a stepbrother, fifteen," continues Leman. "Now we are talking about personalities and relationships that are well formed. To build new relationships among everyone in the family will take time, patience— and maybe some luck."

When Your Birth Order Position Changes

Within a lifetime, a person can experience what it's like to be in several different birth order positions. For instance, Ursula was adopted by her foster parents, the Petermans, when she was six. The family already had two kids, both slightly older than Ursula. When Ursula joined the Peterman family, she was the youngest child. But her birth order experience became more complex when two years later her adoptive mother gave birth to twin boys. Ursula was now a middle child. Ursula now had experienced the birth order circumstances of an adopted, a youngest, and a middle child.

Do you see how complicated birth order theory can be? A child can carry the attributes of one birth order position even as he or she adapts to a new position. The study of birth order can help us understand one another, and ourselves, a little better. The following chapters examine each birth order position and its special aspects. Do you see yourself falling into any typical birth order roles?

Chapter Two

The First Child: Setting an Example

Greta, thirty-nine, is a wealthy stockbroker who lives in New York City. As a child growing up in Michigan, Greta was a firstborn, the oldest child in her family. As is true of many firstborn children, Greta's arrival made her parents very excited. They read all of the latest parenting books. They wanted to do everything just right.

"I guess I was kind of a 'lab rat' for my parents, as the oldest of four children and the only girl," says Greta. "I think I had more rules to follow than my siblings. I was expected to succeed, but so were all my siblings. I have to hand it to my parents, they tried to treat us equally."

Setting the Example

Some firstborns complain that they are expected to set an example for their younger brothers or sisters. They are expected to be responsible and, as a result, often have to grow up a bit sooner than their siblings. For example, when Juanita was four years old, three boys—triplets—joined Juanita's family. "My parents always told me that I should 'set an example' for the boys, which didn't seem fair and still doesn't to this day. My parents were more strict with me than with my brothers," Juanita says. "They were always making up rules for me to follow. If I broke the rules—like, if I didn't do all my chores on time—I was punished, as an 'example' for my younger brothers. Somehow these same rules were lost by the time my brothers were old enough to do chores!"

Extra Responsibilities

Parents often give their firstborn children extra responsibilities. These children are often put in the position of caring for the younger children in the family.

"When I was a teenager, I became the designated baby-sitter," says Juanita. "I didn't have much of a social life because I usually couldn't go out on the weekends."

Trendsetters
The first child helps his or her siblings in a unique way. Firstborns are given the task of "breaking in"

The firstborn child is almost always the first to do things, such as learn to drive.

their parents. In a way, the first child helps the parents learn about being parents, which benefits the younger sisters or brothers.

The oldest child often blazes a trail for the siblings in another way, too. The firstborn is always the first of his or her siblings to do things like walking, learning to ride a bike, and even learning to drive. In essence, the oldest child is a leader among his or her siblings.

Changing Roles

When they are babies, firstborn children are usually graced with their parents' undivided attention and affection. Cameras snap away to capture images of these precious first children. As a result of all this attention, firstborns are likely to have strong egos, sometimes stronger than those of later borns.

But what happens to the firstborn child's birth order rank in the family when more siblings come along?

Pamela

Pamela, a college student and a firstborn in her family, received lots of affection from her parents—at first.

"For the first five years of my life, I was an only child. This was great, as I remember it. My parents gave me all the toys I wanted and focused all of their attention on me. My grandparents and aunts and uncles also adored me and lavished me with attention and gifts."

But when Pamela was six, her parents had another daughter. Two years later they had a son, and, about a year later, another daughter. Pamela remembers that a big change occurred in her life and in her relationship with her parents when her siblings came along.

"The days of getting basically everything I wanted were over. There simply wasn't enough money anymore. Though this was just about 'things,' it made me feel less loved than before.

"Also, I remember that my parents weren't as physically affectionate when my sisters and brother joined the family. Maybe they didn't have

much energy left anymore, with so many kids to raise. They'd say, 'You're a big girl, run along now.' This is a sore spot that still hurts."

Living Up to the Firstborn: Why Can't You Be More Like Your Sister?

When one child is held up as an example for another child to follow, both children are affected—often negatively. Greg is a fifteen-year-old with one brother, Bobby, who is ten.

"I am the oldest of two kids in my family. My mom is always telling Bobby, 'Why can't you be more responsible, like Greg?' or 'Why can't you keep your room clean, like Greg does?' I hate this because it isn't fair to Bobby. She wants Bobby to act more like an older kid when he's not. He's still a little kid. I'm afraid that Bobby will grow up hating me because my mom always compares us."

Diane, a forty-six-year-old concert pianist, was the firstborn daughter as well as the first grandchild on both sides of her family. Like Greg, she was held up as an example for her sister, but it did not eventually result in bad feelings between the two women.

"I had a good home and loving parents. They had, and still have, a very happy relationship. As a child, everything came easily to me. I was trained musically from an early age. I received a lot of individual attention

Parents will sometimes compare siblings to each other, which can cause a lot of tension.

from my parents and grandparents. I remember most of my friends having lots of siblings and that they didn't get to do much that required money. I remember feeling lucky.

"When my sister came along, I loved her but I considered her a pain in the butt. My parents often made me take her along when I played with my friends. When we were older, I was often given the responsibility of baby-sitting her. I hated that then, but today we are close. I think having only one sibling made me appreciate her more."

The Pressure to Succeed

As mentioned earlier, oldest children often carry the burden of their parents' expectations. Because they are always the "big kid" in the family, older children are sometimes pushed ahead by their parents, who expect them to grow up faster than the younger children.

"When I was about five, my brother Jordan was born," says Quinn, age twenty-seven. "I started kindergarten that year and I remember getting dropped off at school and feeling as if I had lost my parents. Today, when I look back, I see that they were sort of giving me away to the school system. I was expected to get good grades from that point on. There was no question about it. I just knew it.

"Meanwhile my parents showered the new baby with affection and attention. They let me take care of the baby, too, and help in little ways, which made me feel important. But I didn't feel like a kid anymore, or I didn't feel like a little kid, which I was. I was no longer the focus of attention, and my parents just expected me to fly on my own."

The Benefits of Being a Firstborn

Every birth order position has its positive and negative points. Firstborn children, so often used to being leaders in their family, tend to be reliable, conscientious, and successful adults. Twenty-one of the first twenty-three astronauts from the United States were firstborn (or only) children. In addition, research shows that a high percentage of firstborn children are doctors, politicians, scientists, and teachers.

Remember Greta, the stockbroker from New York? Today she credits her firstborn birth position with contributing to her sense of self-worth and success in life. "I thank my parents for setting high standards for me. They almost always trusted me to do the right thing, and fortunately, I usually did. Incidentally, I am the first person in my immediate family with a college education!

"Today I am a high achiever with an exciting, high-paying job. I am very, very organized and success-oriented. Funny—even to this day, I still feel the need to please my parents."

Actor and restauranteur Bruce Willis is a famous firstborn.

Common Characteristics of Firstborns

- ◆ Determined
- ◆ High achievers
- ◆ Leaders
- ◆ Organized
- ◆ Parent pleasers
- ◆ Perfectionists
- ◆ Responsible
- ◆ Rule keepers

Famous Firstborns

Lucille Ball	Sigmund Freud
Humphrey Bogart	Brad Pitt
Cher	Sylvester Stallone
Bette Davis	Meryl Streep
Albert Einstein	George Washington
Bridget Fonda	Bruce Willis

Chapter Three | Middle Children: Lost in the Shuffle?

Growing up, Molly was one of ten children, with six older siblings and three younger ones. Today she is married and has five children of her own. To people who study families, this is no surprise: Children from big families often want big families of their own. But middle children, especially in large families, often feel as if they are being overlooked because they don't stand out as "the oldest" or "the youngest."

"I was used to a lot of activity around me all the time but don't recall being an agent in the way things were," Molly recalls. "I was part of a larger shuffle, and maybe it seemed to me as if my problems were not as important as everyone else's. I was shy, soft-spoken, and did not express myself outwardly much at all.

"I didn't spend much one-on-one time with my parents.

For the most part, I was left to my own devices. Luckily, I was imaginative and could amuse myself, and did."

A Place of Their Own

Rather than let themselves become completely "lost in the shuffle" among their siblings, middle-born children like to carve out unique spots for themselves in the family. By the time Molly was a teenager, she was known as the artist in the family, with plans to enter art school when she was eighteen.

In an attempt to gain individuality, middle children are more likely than other children to move away from their family. But not all "middles" create a positive place for themselves in the world. Molly's younger brother Howard also grew up a middle child.

"I left home when I was sixteen," says Howard, now thirty-two. "I just boarded a bus with $68 in savings. My parents made too many rules for me—it was rules, rules, rules at our house. So for about two years I lived on the street. I did drugs, just bummed around. Eventually I got straightened out, but I was pretty messed up for a while."

All Middles Are Not the Same

How could two middle children in the same family have such different behavior? There could be many reasons, but one common cause is that parents sometimes treat the children very differently. Janine, twenty-eight,

Middle-born children often carve out unique spots for themselves within their families.

recalls how her parents set different rules for her siblings and herself.

"I am a middle child, with one older sister and a younger brother. My older sister appeared to have it the hardest, with strict rules to adhere to. I must have been more mellow than my siblings because I didn't have any set rules, like to be home at a certain time on the weekends. However, I never stayed out late, and I always did my homework and chores. On the other hand, my younger brother had a lengthy set of rules to follow as well."

Other Issues

What other issues do middle-born children face? Some middle children are second-born children (the second child in the family birth order). Second-borns are often concerned that they will be upstaged by both the older and younger siblings.

Being Self-Sufficient

In some families, the parents expect their middle-born children to basically take care of themselves. Although this attitude can make a middle child feel neglected at times, it can have positive effects as well. For example, Wendy, who was born when her sister Frieda was eighteen months old and very ill with the measles, feels that being a middle child made her the successful, outgoing person she is today.

"My sister continued to be sick with various health problems throughout her childhood," says Wendy. "My mother used to say, 'I don't have to take care of Wendy, she can take care of herself'. . . so I did! Today I am very independent and a high achiever. I'm also the life of the party."

Following Footsteps

Some middle children feel pressure to be like their brothers or sisters, especially if they are preceded (or followed) by exceptional or talented siblings. Jade, now forty-nine, has two older sisters and two younger sisters. "My sisters were good at everything," she says. "I lived under pressure for years, mainly because my parents expected me to follow in my sisters' footsteps in every way. When I grew up, I think I still did what my parents wanted me to do."

The Peacemaker

Birth order theorists point out that many middle children grow up and enter professions that involve helping or managing people, such as nursing, psychology, and managerial positions. This is probably a reflection of one of the common roles of the middle-born child: that of the peacemaker between siblings.

Bart, twenty-eight, is a middle child, with two older brothers and one younger sister. Like many middle children, Bart was the "negotiator," or peacemaker, among his siblings. "I remember splitting up fights

31

Middle children often act as peace-makers between siblings.

between my older brothers," says Bart. "They were always at each other, competing, wrestling, arguing. I just wanted everybody to get along."

How did Bart's middle-child birth order position influence who he is today? "Today I am a factory manager," Bart explains. "I manage a large group of employees, and a big part of my job is problem solving and resolving conflicts."

Common Characteristics of Middle Children

- Competitive
- Flexible
- Outgoing
- Peacemakers
- People pleasers
- Social

Famous Middle Children

Thomas Jefferson	Groucho Marx
John F. Kennedy	Rosie O'Donnell
Abraham Lincoln	Joan Rivers
Diana, Princess of Wales	

Chapter Four | The Last Child: Attention Seeker?

T he baby of the family . . . everything comes easily to the favored youngest child, right? Not exactly! By the time the youngest child is born, parents are usually more relaxed about child rearing, mostly because they have had practice. On the other hand, youngest children are faced with the challenge of following in their older siblings' footsteps. In addition, last-born children, so used to being called the baby of the family, often have a lot of difficulty becoming independent adults.

Disadvantages

As with all birth order positions, being the last born has its advantages and disadvantages.

Home Alone

Last-born children have to deal with their siblings'

Youngest children are often faced with the pressure of following in their talented older siblings' footsteps.

leaving home before they do. Jeremy remembers the loss he felt when his older brother left home. "I had a brother seven years older than I was. He was my best friend. Even though he was older, I could always confide in him and ask him for advice. I remember missing him so much when he left home and got a job and an apartment in another city. I felt abandoned. It hurt a lot. Suddenly I was an only child."

What's Left for Me?

Ricardo, the youngest of six children in his family, remembers another disadvantage of his birth order position: Youngest children often feel that their parents and relatives have used up all of their attention on the first children and don't have much time or energy left for the last child. "Never in my life did I get to do anything first," Ricardo laments. "My Halloween costumes came from a bin of recycled ones in the basement.

"My folks didn't have time for a sixth kid. No time to put pictures in the photo album, or even to take them at all. The number of pictures of me in my childhood is in the single digits. I also think my parents were older and more tired by the time I came along. They didn't have energy for a young child."

Finding Independence

Typically, it takes last-born children longer than their siblings to strike out on their own and find their own opinions, interests, and paths in life. But Ricardo notes how his siblings gave him a unique edge among his peers. "I had cool older siblings. In grade school, I was ahead of the other kids because I knew about the Beatles, Jimi Hendrix, Joni Mitchell, and the Rolling Stones at an unusually early age. My brother could play the drums, and he taught me how to play. I was a pretty cool second grader."

This early exposure had its drawbacks, too. "Come to think of it," says Ricardo, "I didn't really have the space to develop my own identity and interests—my interests were kind of imposed on me by my older brother and sisters. What they liked, I liked. It wasn't until college, in fact, that I became more independent-minded and realized what my own interests were."

Been There, Done That

Finally, the youngest child often feels that his or her parents don't notice his or her accomplishments because older siblings have already achieved the same things. "I remember how old and mature my sister Bebe seemed when she went to high school, or when another of my siblings learned to drive," says Tina, a college junior. "By the time I had those experiences, they were looked at as no big deal by the other members of my family. I never got to make a splash. Everything had already been done!"

So What's a Kid to Do?

How do last-born children typically compensate for not being first at so many things? How do they make themselves stand out in the family?

Clowning Around

Many last-born children become the "family clown." The role comes easily for many last-born children—at least for those who complain that they are usually not taken seriously by their older siblings.

For example, take Dave, the youngest of four kids. Today he is a friendly, funny "people person" who makes his living as a graphic artist. "I remember being teased a lot as a kid. In a way, I think I was favored—and that is why I was teased a lot—but the teasing hurt. I felt as if nobody took me seriously.

"When I was really young, I remember everybody laughing at cute things I did, like pronouncing words incorrectly," Dave says. "I was the 'funny' kid, and I guess I accepted this role because I am funny as an adult, too. I work in an office where I am known as the wisecracker. I enjoy the role, I've got to admit."

Common Characteristics of Youngest Children

+ Absentminded

+ Affectionate

+ Creative

+ Humorous

+ Late bloomers

+ Outgoing

+ Social

+ Tend to question authority

Famous Youngest Children

Maya Angelou	Thomas Edison
Mariah Carey	Goldie Hawn
Rachel Carson	Diane Sawyer

Singer Mariah Carey is the youngest child in her family.

Chapter Five

Only Children: Centers of Attention or Lonely Onlys?

Responsible, assertive, successful—these are all words commonly associated with only children. Is it just a coincidence that over 50 percent of the United States presidents and over half of today's twelve Supreme Court justices were only (or firstborn) children?

Only children are in a special situation because they have no siblings—no brothers or sisters with whom to share toys or compete for mom and dad's affection. The only child doesn't feel the pressure of measuring up to his or her siblings. However, being an only child can be hard in some ways, too. Only children are often lonely, and all of the responsibility for taking care of their parents falls on them.

"Lonely Onlys"

With no siblings around, it's not surprising that only children frequently feel alone, especially when many of their friends have siblings. Weekends and vacations with the family can be especially tough when there are no other kids around.

"While growing up, I was often lonely," says Hudson, forty-six, an only child. "I wanted a baby brother or sister and would ask for one, only to be rebuked. To compensate, my parents gave me many pets. Many a hamster gave its life to satisfy my need for companionship, not to mention crayfish, frogs, lizards, turtles, two dogs, and several parakeets. I was surrounded by adults, as my grandfather, aunt, uncle, and cousins were just down the street. But still, it didn't matter—I was lonely."

Just Imagine . . .

So how do only children compensate for their loneliness? Many only children, spending hours playing alone and left to their own devices, develop a fertile imagination. Thirty-seven-year-old Milly remembers relying on her imagination for company.

"I was lonely sometimes, and I felt that I was missing out on something. I desperately wanted a brother or sister. I used to cry about it a lot. As a response, I created whole worlds in my imagination—imaginary family, friends, neighborhoods, cities."

It's Mine—All Mine!

Of course, being an only child means that there are no other children around with whom to compete for

Because they have no siblings, only children often benefit from the companionship of pets.

attention, gifts, and love. "In retrospect," Hudson recalls, "I can see I had certain advantages. I never, ever got denied anything (except the pet chimpanzee and penguin). I was really spoiled rotten. As long as I got good grades, I got to do whatever I wanted to do— like paint my room orange and silver. Plus, I got complete control over television viewing."

Milly also remembers getting her own way as a child. "I was a bossy kid. I didn't have to share very often, and my friends envied me for having all my own toys. When a friend came over to play dolls, I told her which doll she could have. And I was very possessive of my friends. I always had one best friend and if she showed disloyalty, I threw a fit. I was definitely used to getting my way. I think the stereotype of the only kid being selfish was true in my case, although I wouldn't call myself selfish as an adult."

Taking Care of Yourself

Much of an only child's early years are spent either alone or in the company of adults instead of other kids. As a result, many only children learn to be very self-sufficient and independent.

"I'm an only child, but I'm not a spoiled brat the way many within society have classified only children," says Denise, forty-two. "I think that being an only child made me very independent. I did and still do enjoy time alone. I don't feel a real need for family or children. I am happily married to a man from a large family. Now I have lots of family around all the time—a big adjustment for me—but kind of fun, too."

"Because I interacted with adults a lot and was often the center of attention, I became very outgoing," says Milly. "I wasn't shy or intimidated by social situations." How does Milly's birth position influence her today? "I am still pretty bossy, and I still seek intense friendships with other people—always looking for that special sister- or brotherlike bond. I am assertive and outgoing today, which I attribute to being an only child."

Carla, twenty-five, describes another positive aspect of being an only child: Being around adults a lot can lead to an early sense of maturity. "The disadvantage for me was that I had no companion around my age to play with. At home I was surrounded by adult relatives who visited often, so as a child, I can remember just hanging out in the kitchen talking to the grown-ups. But in the end, I think this caused me to grow faster mentally than other kids my age. Looking back, I think it wasn't such a bad thing. I was mature, and to this day I am a very responsible person."

Being the Caretaker

Without siblings, only children carry the weight of their parents' expectations and often feel a lot of pressure to

Only children are frequently very mature and comfortable around adults.

succeed. Their thinking is, "If I don't succeed and carry on the family name, who will?"

In addition, only children often feel a strong responsibility toward their parents. As adults, they are more likely than other children to live near their parents. "As my parents age, I will be the only one around to help them," says Denise.

Common Characteristics of Only Children

- ◆ Attention seeking
- ◆ Confident
- ◆ Creative
- ◆ Demanding
- ◆ High achieving
- ◆ Independent

Famous Only Children

Leonardo DiCaprio	**Robin Williams**
Elvis Presley	**Frank Lloyd Wright**
Franklin D. Roosevelt	

Chapter Six

Exceptions to the Rule

Guess what? Birth order isn't everything. Many other factors—such as gender, family size, economic or social position of the family, and, most important, how the child is treated by his or her parents—help make us the people we are today. Below is a list of some factors that can influence the effect of birth order:

- ◆ Gender roles and expectations

- ◆ Marital relationship of parents

- ◆ Parental attitudes and behavior

- ◆ Being the only girl among boys, or the only boy among girls

- The number of years between siblings

- Having an exceptional sibling

- Family size

- Economic situation of family

- Unequal treatment of siblings

Let's look at some of these in greater detail.

The Influence of Gender

In our society, girls are often treated differently than boys. Fortunately, times are changing and many parents today are trying to give male and female children equal treatment. But sexist attitudes and issues regarding sexual identity still exist, and they can—and do—affect a child's developing self.

Pete: Boys Will Be Boys . . . Right?

Pete wasn't like his older brother. He preferred play activity traditionally associated with females. He and his younger sister, Sally, were practically inseparable. They spent hours playing with dolls.

Pete didn't have many male friends. The neighborhood boys and his brother, Bryan, called him a sissy. This hurt Pete's feelings and had lasting effects on his self-esteem. Pete wanted to have friends and fit in. But he felt like an outsider.

"I had an older brother who did the traditionally boy things: baseball, football, rough sports. I didn't relate to these things and felt as if I had let him down as a brother.

"The younger brother is expected to be like the older brother, I think. But I was different and felt alone in my wants and needs. I bonded more with my sister. I didn't want to play cowboys and Indians with Bryan. I wanted to have a Barbie fashion show with Sally."

Tristine: One Sister, Five Brothers

Tristine was a middle child in a family of five children. But another factor influenced her childhood development as much as, if not more than, being a middle child: Out of the six children, Tristine was the only girl.

"My older two brothers scared off any boy who was interested in dating me. I was taught to be tough and I was a tomboy. In my family, I am the levelheaded child, the one who tries to fix everyone else's problems. Today, when one of my brothers has a problem, he comes to me."

Parental Behavior

The way that parents treat their children, as well as

Being the only girl among boys, or the only boy among girls, can affect a child's development.

each other, has an enormous impact on the development of children. A rocky relationship between parents can lead to overall family unhappiness that affects all members. In addition, some children, particularly only children, feel compelled to stop their parents from fighting, and this pressure can create problems that last long into adulthood.

Relationships Between Parents

When parents fight, they often devote most of their attention to their personal problems, leaving little time and energy for their children. Will, a last-born child with three siblings, remembers growing up with fighting parents. "When I was young, my parents were going through a very difficult time. They had money and relationship problems. I didn't feel there was any affection for me during those younger years.

"I didn't get the piano or guitar lessons that my siblings got. I don't remember outings to the zoo with my parents or having friends over for birthday or slumber parties. My parents were preoccupied, I guess. They were spread thin and didn't have the time or energy for all of their kids."

The Complexity of Family Dynamics

Family situations can be extremely complex—so complex, in fact, that predicting how each child will turn out is virtually impossible.

Jim and Auden

Jim and his older brother, Auden, were raised by parents who frequently fought in front of their children. Plus, their mom was mentally ill. The differences in personality and attitude between Jim and Auden were as much a result of their parents' behavior as their birth positions.

"Our childhood home was kind of a battlefield," remembers Jim. "My parents were always fighting. Auden became kind of a problem for my parents. And they didn't discipline him or even spend that much time with him, so he only got worse.

"I felt like a forgotten child. I remember trying to be good. I studied in my room and tried to be quiet. I didn't want to be the source of any more arguing. I was dreadfully afraid that my parents would divorce.

"When I was six and Auden was ten, my parents divorced. My mother cut off all contact between my father and us. Meanwhile, my mother was becoming more and more unstable. She would just disappear for days at a time, sometimes weeks. When my mom was gone, I felt like the 'mother' to my irresponsible older brother. Somebody had to keep it together. Eventually, my grandparents got custody of my brother and me.

"Today, I am still the responsible one. I hold a good job and live in a nice house. Though my

relationship with my parents is very strained today, my brother and I are close."

Caught in the Middle: Jana

As an only child of parents with many relationship problems, Jana was often caught in the middle of her parents' problems. "Though I was an only child, I think the main disadvantages in my life had to do with the particular misery in my family. My parents did not have a happy marriage, and they put me in the middle. Both vied for my sympathy and used me as a confidante. This still happens, and I resent it. I don't want and never wanted to be in the middle of my parents' relationship."

Dealing with a Gifted Sibling

Most children, regardless of their birth order position, find it hard to follow in the steps of an exceptional sibling.

Esther

Esther is a high school sophomore with below-average grades. She is kind of shy and has a hard time making friends. Her sister Sandra is a high school senior. Sandra gets all A's, is on the school honor roll, and was voted class president.

"It is so-oooo hard having a popular sister," says Esther, "though I would never tell her that.

She already has a big head. I wouldn't want it to get any bigger. It just seems like my sister has it easy. She wins all of these awards and stuff and everybody thinks she's so great. I try hard, but I can never measure up to her.

"My parents give both Sandra and me $25 for every A we get on our report cards. Obviously, my sister has a lot more money than I do in her savings account. It isn't fair, you know? I wish my parents would treat us the same, but they don't."

Psychological Birth Order

What is "psychological birth order"? Allen is a good example of what some people call a "psychological only child." Although Allen is the youngest in his family, with two older brothers, there is a huge age difference between Allen and his siblings. As a result, as a young child Allen played alone at home, almost as if there were no other children present. By the time Allen was seven, both of his brothers had left home for college.

"I am the youngest of three boys. Tony is fourteen years older than I am, and Rick is twelve years older than I am. When I was born, my brothers were already 'big kids.' They didn't want to hang around with a baby. Later I got my own friends, but I do remember those early years of feeling left out.

"My brothers are good friends with each other. They did everything together as kids, and they continue to do so today. Tony and Rick both went to the same college and lived in the same dorm for a while. They were both on the college tennis team, both majored in business, and today they live two blocks from one another in the same town.

"I took a different road in life. I work as a commercial artist for a magazine. They think I'm weird—too artistic or something. We can't relate to one another very well. It makes me sad. I wish we were closer—they are my brothers, after all."

How Can Parents Help?

"When you become aware of each of your children's birth order issues, identify them when they arise, and learn how to intervene, you can really make a difference in your children's lives," says psychologist and author Meri Wallace.

"You must also learn which of your own behaviors contribute to your children's problems and how to avoid them. Once you understand the issues and become actively involved by using a positive phrase or action, you can help your children to overcome their problems."

Parents can also help to close the gaps caused by differences in birth order in a family by creating a noncompetitive environment in their home.

No matter what size a family is, parents should encourage kids to be individuals.

When Moesha Johnson was born, she had one older brother, Angus, who was four years old. Newborn baby Moesha needed lots of attention from her parents, but Angus needed attention, too. After all, he still felt like the baby of the family— he was used to lots of attention. Moesha's parents were careful to give baby Moesha and Angus their own, individual "special" time.

As Moesha and Angus grew older, the Johnsons were careful not to load Angus with extra responsibility, such as making him "set an example" or even baby-sit for Moesha. They also made sure that Moesha felt free to develop her own interests and to express herself. Each child's individuality was acknowledged.

In other words, Moesha and Angus's parents encouraged their children to be individuals, with their own unique talents, interests, strong points, and weaknesses. They gave their children equal treatment.

No Magic Formula

Why does your big brother always grab the biggest piece of cake? Why is your best friend, an only child, so darn bossy? And why does your little sister tell those silly jokes all the time?

Unfortunately, there is no magic formula for understanding human behavior. Fortunately, however, when we are aware of the possible effects of birth order, we can understand others, and ourselves, a little bit better.

Glossary

absentminded   Lost in thought and unaware of one's surroundings or actions.

assertive   Characterized by confident actions and speech.

attributes   Characteristics; traits.

birth order   The order in which children are born; birth position.

birth position   The position (first, middle, last, only) that a child occupies in a family.

compensate   To make up for; to supply with an equivalent.

drawback   Disadvantage; negative aspect of something.

ego   The self, especially in relation to others and to the world.

fertile   Productive; inventive.

flexible   Able to adapt to varied environments and situations.

genetics   The study of genes (the material that passes on traits from one generation to the next).

gifted   Exceptionally talented.

outgoing   Openly friendly; extroverted.

perfectionistic   Very demanding of oneself; unaccepting of and dissatisfied with any aspect of one's behavior that is less than perfect.

possessive   Wanting to own or dominate people or things.

preoccupied   Lost in thought; distracted.

self-esteem   Confidence in and respect for oneself.

self-sufficient   Independent; capable of surviving without the help of others.

well-adjusted   Well-balanced; well-adapted to most situations.

Where to Go for Help

In the United States

Early Childhood Center
8730 Alden Drive, Room E-105
Los Angeles, CA 90048
(310) 855-3576
Web site: http://www.choicemail.com/warmline
E-mail: info@warmline.com

Families Anonymous
P.O. Box 3475
Culver City, CA 90231-3475
(800) 736-9805 or
(310) 815-8010
Web site: http://www.familiesanonymous.org
E-mail: famanon@familiesanonymous.org

In Canada

Family and Community Support Services
Association of Alberta
1 Alexandra Park
Leduc, AB T9E 4C4
(780) 980-7109
Web site: http://www.city.leduc.ed.ce

Family Service Association of Metropolitan
Toronto
22 Wellesley Street East
Toronto, ON M4Y 1G3
(416) 595-9618
Web site: http://www.fsatoronto.com

Web Sites

Dealing with Sibling Rivalry
http://www.choicemail.com/warmline/skills14.html

Family Skills: Managing Sibling Rivalry
http://www.gartland.com/phoenix/95-7/7-sibli.html

Prevent Sibling Rivalry
http://www.parentsoup.com/challenges/sibrivalry0798

Sibling Rivalry
http://www.parallaxweb.com/parenting.sibriv.html

For Further Reading

Adler, Alfred. *What Life Should Mean to You.* Boston: Little, Brown, 1931.

Forer, Lucille K., Ph.D, with Henry Still. *The Birth Order Factor: How Your Personality Is Influenced by Your Place in the Family.* New York: David McKay Company, Inc., 1976.

Leman, Kevin, M.D. *The Birth Order Book: Why You Are the Way You Are.* New York: Dell Publishing, 1985.

Sulloway, Frank J. *Born to Rebel: Birth Order, Family Dynamics, and Creative Lives.* New York: Pantheon Books, 1996.

Wallace, Meri. *Birth Order Blues: How Parents Can Help Their Children Meet the Challenges of Birth Order.* Markham, ON: Fitzhenry & Whiteside, 1999.

Index

About the Author

Katherine Krohn has written many books for young readers, as well as news articles and fiction. Originally from Germany, Ms. Krohn now lives in the Pacific Northwest.

Photo Credits

Cover shot by Ira Fox. All interior shots by Maura Boruchow except for p. 25 © Popperfoto/ Archive Photos and p. 39 © Reuters/Fred Prouser/ Archive Photos.

Layout

Geri Giordano